Original title:
Life's Answers Are Mysterious at Best

Copyright © 2025 Creative Arts Management OÜ
All rights reserved.

Author: Evan Hawthorne
ISBN HARDBACK: 978-1-80566-287-7
ISBN PAPERBACK: 978-1-80566-582-3

Mysteries Laced with Hope

In the fridge, a snack appears,
Wondering if it's just my fears.
Leftovers dance in a strange ballet,
Will they haunt me or save the day?

A sock disappears with flair and style,
Leaving behind an empty tile.
Is it hiding in some secret place?
Or just off to run in a sock race?

The Puzzle of Existence

Jigsaw pieces shaped like a shoe,
I thought they'd fit, but that's not true!
The corners are lost, and edges fray,
Just like my socks that decided to play.

A puzzle box, with no lid to close,
I shake it gently, what do I pose?
A cat with glasses trying to solve,
The riddle of why my soup won't evolve.

Secrets of the Inner Cosmos

A starfish counts its little toes,
While pondering why the river flows.
In the depths of socks, strange secrets hide,
Like dust bunnies that giggle and glide.

Cosmic cookies fall from the sky,
With chocolate chips shaped like a pie.
And aliens wonder, what's with the cheese?
As I ponder, they say, 'Just take it with ease!'

The Edge of Understanding

Why does toast always hit the floor?
I must have stepped out of a door!
With buttered hopes upon my shoe,
The floor claims victory, it's true!

I ask the cat what's on her mind,
Her gaze says, 'Human, you are blind.'
So I blame the universe's push,
For leaving me in this mad rush.

Labyrinth of Life's Paradoxes

In a maze made of socks and keys,
Every turn is a new disease.
Do I take the ice cream or the pie?
While pondering, I can only sigh.

My plants whisper secrets at night,
But when I water, they just take flight.
With each green leaf, a riddle grows,
In the soil, more questions pose.

The Allure of the Uncharted

A map drawn with crayons and dreams,
Leads to wonders and silly schemes.
What's beyond the edge of my yard?
Where mysteries linger, unbarred.

Chasing shadows that flicker and dance,
In a world that offers little chance.
Perhaps a dragon or a lost shoe,
All the answers wave 'Hey, how do you do?'

Echoes in the Silence

In the quiet, I hear a sneeze,
Maybe it's just a gentle breeze.
Questions float like balloons that cling,
To answers that dance and never sing.

Finding wisdom in a banana peel,
Or perhaps a cat who's made a meal.
Life chuckles as I scratch my head,
While mystery whispers, 'Go to bed!'

When Stars Collide

A comet tripped on a moonlit beam,
And spilled its glitter, what a scene!
Galaxies danced in a clumsy waltz,
As planets laughed at their silly faults.

A wink from Saturn, a giggle from Mars,
As they clink glasses full of candy bars.
In the cosmos, the humor's not sly,
Stars collide, but they never say why!

Veils of Fate and Fortune

In a world of twists and turns,
Fortunes dance like playful fawns.
We chase them down with hopes and yearns,
Yet every prize still wears a yawn.

A rabbit's foot, a lucky charm,
Will never save you from the fall.
With every step, there's just alarm,
But laughter echoes through it all.

The dice may roll, the cards might play,
Yet chaos reigns in every game.
We ask, we guess, we hope, we sway,
But what's the point? It's all the same!

So here we are, with fate's embrace,
A comical ballet of chance.
With clumsy steps, we find our place,
And in the farce, we laugh and dance.

The Hidden Pathways of Tomorrow

Tomorrow comes, or so they say,
But really, who can ever tell?
With tangled roads that twist and sway,
What's up ahead? Who knows too well?

A coin flip here, a map gone wrong,
We think we're clever, oh so slick.
But every plan can't last too long,
And fate just laughs with every trick.

So here I stand, with shoes untied,
A sign that points in every way.
Yet all my thoughts, they just collide,
As stumbles lead me into play.

With every step, uncertainty,
Is coffee spilled or magic brewed?
Tomorrow's paths are hard to see,
And through the fog, we're quite bemused.

Unraveling Threads of Thought

Threads of thought, they weave and spin,
A tangled mess with every pause.
We pull and tug, but where to begin?
While reason chuckles, just because.

With every question, all's a blur,
A riddle wrapped in silly jokes.
We ponder hard, yet minds deter,
While wisdom hides behind the pokes.

Trying to decipher the grand scheme,
Like finding socks in a washing floor.
Each answer's just a wild dream,
As laughter bursts through every door.

So here's to thoughts that will not quit,
A comedy of errors at best.
With tangled webs, we still commit,
To finding fun in all the rest.

The Art of Unknowing

In the gallery of what we lack,
Uncertainty hangs on each wall.
We paint in shades of bright and black,
And laugh at how we clearly fall.

With scribbles here and doodles there,
We ponder questions, oh so grand.
Yet every answer's light as air,
Like tickling fate's supportive hand.

Every puzzle piece we find,
Seems made for just the other guy.
The more we seek, the more we're blind,
As jokes are tossed and giggles fly.

The art of not knowing is key,
A playful dance on mystery's floor.
With each mistake, we find some glee,
And laugh together, wanting more.

The Unfolding Map of Wonder

A map stretched wide, with colors bright,
Where X marks spots of pure delight.
Yet when you ask the way to go,
It often leads to the oddest show.

Cacti wearing hats, a cat that sings,
A dog that dances, and other things.
Instructions scribbled in crayon and fun,
Your journey's just begun, oh what a run!

But hold your compass, it's quite a joke,
For at the crossroads, rocks seem to poke.
Turn left for treasure, right for a prank,
In search of wisdom—be sure to thank!

So when you roll the dice, just cheer,
The paths of quests are never clear.
Each twist and turn a giggle or jest,
The secret, my friend, is in the quest.

Tapestry of Unsolved Tales

Threads weave stories, bright and bold,
Some warm and fuzzy, others cold.
Behind each stitch, a grin or frown,
True mysteries hide in velvet gown.

A sock with stripes that lost its mate,
Or shoes that dance before it's late.
What do they mean, those mismatched pairs?
A cosmic joke? No one compares!

The weaver laughs, with wisdom old,
As each new twist just brightens gold.
In tangled yarns, odd shapes abound,
Seek less the answers, more the sound.

So gather round, let's share a yarn,
Of tales absurd that tease and charm.
In every knot, a pun will dwell,
Life's grand parade—a circus swell!

The Allure of Uncertainty

In a game of chance, I take my seat,
Rolling the dice, it's quite the feat.
What's in the box? A riddle, a treat?
Could it be sweet—or just some beet?

With paths obscure and signs out of whack,
I step on a snail, hear laughter crack.
An octopus plays cards on the floor,
While a toaster sings—who could ask for more?

What good's a plan when curves get tossed?
Perhaps the map has been embossed.
With answers few and guesses galore,
Uncertainty knocks, and we can't ignore!

So let's embrace this playful mess,
Make friends with doubt, it's for the best.
For in the haze of whimsy and chance,
Is where we learn to truly prance.

Fragments of a Shattered Mirror

Pieces scattered, gleaming bright,
Festive shards in morning light.
What's reflected, a face unknown,
Smiles and frowns, a riot grown.

A mirror sings, but cracks do show,
Each fragment holds a quirky glow.
What's truth today may flip and spin,
In this funhouse, chaos begins.

Duck in on Tuesday, fly out on Friday,
Jump through time in a wild ballet.
A puzzle shuffled, how very neat,
Who knew confusion could taste so sweet?

Embrace the splinters, dance on the edge,
Sing with the voices, make the pledge.
For in the shards lies laughter's art,
Together we forge, in folly's heart.

Dance of the Veiled

What's underneath the silly veil?
A sock, a spoon, a busted tail!
Shuffling feet and clumsy twirls,
Our hidden truths are laughing girls.

Beneath the moon and wiggly lights,
We spin around, lose all our sights.
A wig, a hat, a pair of shoes,
It's hard to tell who's who—we muse!

In crooked lines, we twine and bend,
The mystery? It's just pretend!
With punchlines tossed and giggles shared,
Our funniest thoughts have all declared.

When shadows creep in over the floor,
We dance and leap, who's keeping score?
A twirl, a whirl, we stumble through,
What's underneath? Just me and you!

The Heart's Uncharted Waters

A map of feelings, lost and tossed,
With X's marking where love's crossed.
Navigating through the ups and downs,
Where mermaids dance and flounders frown.

A boat that leaks and sails that flop,
Love's compass spins, it just won't stop!
With jellyfish and dancing crabs,
Our hearts can't help but play their jabs.

In waters deep, where secrets swim,
We dive right in—oh, what a whim!
With laughter bubbling up like foam,
Who needs a map? We'll find our home!

The current pulls, we laugh and splash,
In every wave, there's joy to dash.
So raise a toast to all our fails,
In uncharted seas, we write our tales!

Shadows of Forgotten Realities

In this room of echoes lost,
We dance with ghosts that pay the cost.
A sock here, a shoe there,
Forgotten dreams drift through the air.

Ticklish feelings and haunting plays,
We giggle at our silly ways.
With shadows swaying in the light,
We trip and laugh through endless night.

"Did I leave my mind in the fridge?"
"Or maybe it's stuck on a bridge?"
Our whispers tickle forgotten tales,
In shadows, we've unleashed the gales.

So let's embrace the missed delights,
As giggles dance with silly sights.
For in this maze of lost replay,
We find the joy in lost and stray!

Secrets Beneath the Waves

Underneath the glimmery foam,
Are sneaky crabs making their home.
With giggles buried in the sand,
We uncover treasures, oh so grand!

A beach ball rolls, truth starts to slip,
The ocean's laughter takes a dip.
With waves that tickle our sandy toes,
The secret's out—everyone knows!

What hides below? A fishy joke!
A seahorse dance, then watch it poke.
With sandy hands and brightened eyes,
We search for pearls, where laughter lies!

So splash about, and let them see,
The secrets play, so couldn't we?
Beneath the waves, our fears unravel,
In every tide, we find the travel!

The Labyrinth of Wonder

In mazes wide, I search for clues,
Each twist and turn, I just confuse.
The paths are silly, I can't deny,
I chase my tail, oh me, oh my!

With every sign, a riddle blooms,
A dancing squirrel, it just assumes.
Lost in thought, my compass spins,
Where is the exit? It's all just whims!

A blindfolded cat and a jester's hat,
They giggle at me, 'Look where you're at!'
I take a leap, I trip and fall,
But laughter echoes, amidst it all!

So here I stand, with a grin so wide,
In this amusing ride, I take in stride.
The twists may baffle, the turns may jest,
But in the fun, I find my rest.

Unraveled Threads of Fate

A sweater's back with pulled-out yarn,
Stitches loose, it looks forlorn.
The pattern's gone, but that's okay,
I wear it proudly, come what may!

The weaver's lost, forgot to tie,
Yet here I sit, I won't deny.
The fabric laughs, with quirky seams,
In a tangled dance of silly dreams!

Each thread a tale, each loop a tease,
Obscure designs, that aim to please.
With every tug, a chuckle grows,
And humor hides in tangled throes!

So let's embrace this jumbled fate,
With every knot, we can relate.
For in the mess lies art so grand,
A wacky journey, both light and planned!

Dance of the Unknown

A waltz with shadows, it starts to sway,
The music's strange, but I'll replay.
With every step, I lose my shoes,
Tripping over what not to choose!

The floor is wobbling, we're out of tune,
A polka's played by a laughing moon.
I spin and twirl, the world's a jest,
Embracing chaos, it feels the best!

In this ballroom of delighted whims,
I dance with doubts, I laugh at sins.
A partner's sought in euphoria's trance,
With each wrong move, we just enhance!

So join the jig, let worries fade,
In this wild dance, no masquerade.
For when we stumble, we find delight,
In wacky steps, our spirits take flight!

Veils of Perception

Wearing glasses of kaleidoscope hues,
I see the world with silly views.
A cupcake's pink and sneakers are green,
The squirrel wears pants, it's quite a scene!

Through tinted lenses, truths are fun,
A playful spin, we laugh and run.
With every shade, a giggle grows,
What's real, who knows? Who even knows?

Reflections change as I tilt my head,
The cat's in a cape, the dog's in bed.
Each view a puzzle, it's quite absurd,
Words like fireworks, they whizz and blurred!

So let's unmask what's hid from sight,
In the zany chaos, all feels right.
Embrace the playful, the quirky, and strange,
For in the laughter, we find the change!

Threads of Serendipity

In the fabric of fate, I lost my thread,
Searching for wisdom, tripped on my spread.
Witty little signs, like socks left alone,
Turned my coffee into a wise old scone.

A cat in a hat said, 'You must not fret!'
As I chased a rainbow with my shopping cart vet.
Each twist of the yarn, a laugh or a plight,
Making sense of nonsense in the dim morning light.

The Maze of Time's Guidance

I wandered in circles, a clock on the wall,
Chasing my shadow as it began to fall.
Why do paths twist like spaghetti on fire?
Even the GPS turned into a liar.

With each step I took, I laughed at my fate,
A sign said 'This Way' but I chose to wait.
Outwitted by pigeons who seem to know best,
Life's riddles unfold like a chicken's nest.

Chasing Shadows of Clarity

I caught a glimpse of sense in the clouds,
But it teased me away, hiding in crowds.
Like trying to catch smoke with a butterfly net,
Each flutter unravels, making me fret.

In search of the answer that plays hide and seek,
I found only giggles from a wise old cheek.
Yet in the confusion, I toss up my hands,
A punchline awaits in the mess of life's plans.

The Unsolved Symphony

Notes dance wildly, off the beat,
Clocks tick softly, can't find their feet.
A cat plays piano, what a sight,
While socks seem to vanish, taking flight.

Banjos and banter echo through space,
Every odd tune, a comical chase.
We search for answers, like lost keys,
Only to find we just need to sneeze.

So grab a friend, and join the spree,
Tap your toes to this kooky melody.
In the chaos of chords, joy we'll glean,
It's all a riddle, or so it seems!

Jokes hidden between every note,
Like a squirrel that learned to float.
Fancy some laughter? Just listen near,
Life's just a show; let's give a cheer!

A Journey Through Fog

Through the mist I stumbled, a monkey in shoes,
Lost in the riddle of yesterday's snooze.
Each turn brought a chuckle, a riddle or pop,
As foggy as marshmallows, I just couldn't stop.

With whispers of wisdom danced in the gloom,
I asked for directions, got laughter and zoom.
In the maze of the clouds, clarity might sway,
But laughter is key to unlock any day.

The Mask of Time

Tick-tock whispers in a cheeky tone,
Wearing a mask that's fully blown.
Yesterday's socks have gone astray,
Tomorrow's breakfast? Who's to say!

A jester dances with a crooked grin,
What's behind door three? Let's spin!
Mysteries cloak the sands of the hour,
Like a wizard's tricks with a sneaky power.

Behind each corner, a giggle hides,
While clocks play tag on whimsical rides.
If you think you know, you're quite the fool,
Throw on a mask; let's bend the rule!

Have a laugh with the wrinkles of fate,
Join in the fun; don't hesitate!
In the carnival of time, we leap,
What's certain is nothing, but the fun we keep!

Enigmatic Journeys Within

A suitcase packed with dreams and glee,
Yet socks don't fit; I wonder why me?
Off to the land of the unplanned,
With a map that's drawn in crayon sand.

Riding a unicorn on a bus,
With nacho cheese—oh, what a fuss!
Under the rainbow, we giggle and sway,
As the answers play hide-and-seek all day.

Each twist and turn, a riddle or jest,
Where pillows talk and invite for a rest.
Let's dance with shadows, embrace the weird,
In a spiral of questions, our laughter's cleared.

So grab your hat, let's zoom far and wide,
The truth's just a punchline we haven't tried.
On this journey, we'll sing and spin,
Throw caution aside; let the fun begin!

Threads of the Unknowable

Woven in colors, vibrant and bright,
Tangled in twirls, like a kite in flight.
Yarns of the awkward rolling around,
With a knitting needle that's lost, yet found.

Spinning tales like cats chase tails,
In a world of waffles and whispered wails.
Pulling at threads, what will we reap?
A quilt of confusion, or just a heap?

Frogs in tuxedos jumping in glee,
Their laughter echoes like a banjo spree.
Every stitch a mystery, every knot a joke,
In the fabric of chaos, the fun awoke.

So grab a thread, let's stitch the plot,
In a quilt of giggles, give it a shot.
With each twist and turn, we'll laugh and play,
Finding joy in the threads that lead us astray!

Questions in the Twilight

Why does toast always land face down?
Is it fate or a kitchen clown?
Do socks in the dryer have a plot?
Or just dance until they're caught?

If cats could talk, what would they say?
"More tuna, less of this ballet!"
When birds forget the words to their song,
Do they just wing it all day long?

Why does cereal get soggy so fast?
Is breakfast just a race, a blast?
When plumbers fight, is it with wrenches?
Or do they just engage in strange drenches?

In dreams, do we find the questions we seek?
Or just visit a realm that's quite bleak?
Let's laugh at these queries, no need to fret,
For in the absurd, we may find a bet.

Riddles of the Heart

Why do hearts skip just like a stone?
When we trip over words, are we alone?
Do butterflies feel a real sensation,
Or just party in hearts' celebration?

Why do lovers whisper things at night?
Is it secrets or just pure delight?
When two souls collide in a dance so sweet,
Do they plan a future or just a tweet?

If chocolates are sweet, then why the weight?
Are they a gift or a tempting fate?
When hugs turn awkward, what's the right cue?
Do we laugh it off or bid adieu?

With odd little riddles, we frolic and roam,
In the garden of hearts, we feel right at home.

Beneath the Surface of Illusions

Are clouds just cotton candy in disguise?
Floating around with sugary lies?
Why do shadows play tag in the sun?
Is it a secret game just for fun?

When mirrors reflect our quirky side,
Is it comedy or irony we hide?
Does laughter echo in puddles of rain?
Or is puddle-jumping just part of the game?

What do fish think when they swim in schools?
Are they studying math or just playing fools?
If rocks could speak, what tales would they spin?
Of adventures past or where they've been?

In this carnival of life, let's peek and explore,
Finding laughter in riddles and so much more.

In Search of Hidden Realms

What's hidden beneath the bed in the night?
Dust bunnies plotting their daring flight?
If carrots could talk, would they squelch their fear?
Of becoming a salad, their end might be near!

Why do chairs creak when nobody's around?
Is it ghosts trying out their new sound?
When the fridge hums a late-night tune,
Is it serenading the pale, full moon?

If clouds have dreams, what do they behold?
Sunny skies or thunderstorms bold?
When clocks tick loudly, do they conspire?
In shadows of seconds, what do they aspire?

In the search for the strange, let humor take flight,
For in hidden realms, we find pure delight.

Songs of the Unsought

In a world of question marks,
Cats chase tails, like silly sparks.
Wondering why the sky's so blue,
While socks disappear, and that's not new.

We search for truths in tiny dreams,
Like finding spoons in soup it seems.
Questions bubble in a pot,
Who knew my goldfish is so hot?

I ask my plants about their thoughts,
They whisper back in tangled knots.
The toaster laughs when I despair,
It burns my bagel like it's a dare.

So here we dance on whims and fates,
With silly hats and wobbly skates.
Embrace the riddles, jokes, and jest,
And nibble wisdom, it's the best!

Reflections on Hidden Journeys

On the path where flip-flops squeak,
I ponder if a rubber chicken can speak.
With every step, more questions sprout,
Why does cereal always end in doubt?

I visited a sage at dawn's first light,
He offered cookies, said they're insight.
"Why the world spins?" I asked with a grin,
He laughed hard and said, "Just dive in!"

So I wander with my mismatched shoes,
Searching for answers, juggling blues.
The squirrels giggle as I trip and fall,
Maybe they know, but won't tell at all.

Through giggles and grumbles, we roam afar,
In search of wisdom, beneath a star.
With quirks and chuckles, roll with the quest,
Adventure awaits, and it's a jest!

Whims of the Unknown

With a hat made of pudding, I strut with pride,
In a land where questions take a wild ride.
Do ducks think about their quacky fate?
Or is their world just filled with plate?

I zoom on a pogo, past a prancing cat,
While pondering where the lost keys sat.
A llama yells, "What's your plan?" with glee,
I say, "To find answers, not just tea!"

As I dance with shadows in a marshmallow field,
Thoughts bubble like soda that never gets sealed.
Can lost socks bloom like flowers of delight?
Or is that a question that's way out of sight?

So I twirl with the moon and waltz with the breeze,
Wondering if ants ever feel at ease.
With laughter and whimsy, let's take on the quest,
In the laughter of questions, we are truly blessed!

An Odyssey of Questions

In a boat made of paper, I sail the unknown,
Asking if fish ever feel quite alone.
Why do pancakes flip, yet never grow wings?
And what do you call a cat that sings?

I met a giraffe on a unicycle ride,
Beneath a sun where conspiracy hides.
"Why do we giggle? What makes us cheer?"
He paused, then said, "Just grab another beer!"

Through forests of puzzles and rivers of doubt,
I chase after fables, wandering about.
Is chocolate a fruit? Does laughter expand?
These questions are goofy, but oh so grand!

On this journey of quirks and delightful mishaps,
We'll solve the riddles and share silly claps.
Embrace the unknown, with a wink and a jest,
For answers are treasures, but questions are best!

A Tapestry of Queries

Why do socks vanish in the wash?
Is it a sock thief or just a posh?
Do fish ever get lost in their bowl?
Or do they giggle at our role?

Do birds really know the way to the sun?
Or are they just having fun on the run?
What if the moon is a giant cheese?
That makes the mice dance with ease!

If cats can see ghosts, what do they say?
Do they hold secret meetings each day?
Is laughter just a bubble of cheer?
Or an echo of a joke we can't hear?

Are we all but jigs in a cosmic joke?
Made to giggle, awaken, and poke?
With questions spinning like tops in the breeze,
We laugh at the mysteries that tease.

Intrigue in Every Breath

Why do we trip when there's no one around?
Do floorboards conspire to bring us down?
Does the universe chuckle in code?
Or am I just clumsy on this road?

Do clouds hold secrets, floating with grace?
What are they whispering in soft, fluffy space?
If laughter is music, who wrote the score?
And how do we dance without knowing more?

Are shoes just prisons for our feet?
What happens to them when we retreat?
Did the forks conspire to make me a mess?
Or was it just hunger? I must confess!

If mirrors could talk, what would they say?
Would they spill secrets or just lead us astray?
In the rhythm of quirks, we find our fun,
Questions abound, like a race never run.

The Secret in the Stillness

Why do we yawn when boredom is near?
Is it our body trying to steer?
When dogs chase tails, what's their plan?
Are they training for something we don't understand?

If chairs have feelings, do they get shy?
Or just grumble beneath us, oh my!
Do toasters dream of dancing bread?
Or do they think, 'I'd rather be wed'?

Why do cats knock things off the shelf?
Is it an artist's expression of self?
When autumn leaves tumble and fall,
Are they playing tag, or just having a ball?

In silence, we ask more than we find,
With quirky thoughts that dance in the mind.
Each chuckle a ripple, each smile a thread,
In the stillness, we laugh until we're fed.

Questions that Linger

If I sneeze, does the planet get tilted?
Or does the universe just feel slightly spilt?
Can plants argue over who's tallest?
Or do they support each other, the galliest?

Do bugs think we're giants above?
Or are we just part of their world they love?
When coffee spills, is it an art?
Or just a reminder I'm not that smart?

Do shoes have opinions on where we go?
Or do they just follow to steal the show?
If whispers could shout, what would they scream?
Would they reveal the truth in a dream?

In questions we linger, in giggles we sway,
Embracing the chaos, come what may.
For life's a dance of doubts and of fun,
Laughing along till the day is done.

Uncharted Waters of the Heart

In a sea of socks and mismatched shoes,
I navigate feelings, dodging the blues.
The map is a riddle, no compass in sight,
Yet I paddle along, cackling with fright.

Love's a fish that wiggles and flops,
Sometimes it swims, sometimes it stops.
With waves of confusion splashing my face,
I wonder if boats were the right choice of space.

I set sail at dawn with a breakfast of toast,
But who knew the tides could be quite such a boast?
The ocean is laughing, it dances and plays,
While I stew in my thoughts, lost in the maze.

Yet through all the chaos, I'm finding some cheer,
For in joy's little whirlpools, I'm learning to steer.
In uncharted waters, I find my own art,
Navigating feelings, a true work of heart.

The Silent Song of Questions

Whispers of doubt float around my head,
Like socks in the dryer, where'd they all tread?
I ask my reflection, it just shrugs away,
Is this how we ponder on a lazy day?

Like a cat in the sunbeams, I lounge and I sigh,
Where did I put that delightful pie?
The mysteries woo me, a thrilling tune,
While I juggle my worries and balance a spoon.

Are pigeons just spies in a bird disguise?
They flap and they coo, oh what a surprise!
These silent tunes leave me scratching my head,
While plotting my next snack, or a nap instead.

In the end, it's all laughter that fills up the air,
The song of confusion—a carnival fair!
With questions still swirling, I'll dance 'til I drop,
Laughing at answers that bubble and pop.

Mysteries Lurking in Plain Sight

Hidden among the mundane and meek,
I search for the answers, they're hard to sneak.
Like a sock in the wash is an old coin's delight,
Some things just vanish, oh what a sight!

My cat stares at shadows, pondering deep,
Is he dreaming of mice, or counting his sleep?
Whiskers twitching, an enigma grand,
Sometimes I feel like I don't understand.

The toaster pops bread, but why's it so loud?
Does it think it's a singer, all proud in this crowd?
With a laugh and a grin, I'll question it all,
As I trip on my dreams, like a child at a ball.

In this buffet of quirks, we feast and we play,
Chasing odd riddles that dance in the fray.
So let's raise our glasses to wonders unknown,
For truth's just a giggle, in a world we've outgrown.

An Odyssey of Open Doors

Each door that I pass leads to questions anew,
One's labeled 'Socks,' another 'Cat Coo.'
I ponder my choices with a wink and a grin,
Why open a door when there's chaos within?

The kitchen's a maze where the spices collide,
I venture in boldly, the fridge has my guide.
But what's that strange sound from under the rug?
A sock-monster lurking, or just a small bug?

In rooms full of laughter, I dance 'til I drop,
With quirky mischief that never will stop.
A symphony plays with each creak and each squeak,
Exploring these hallways, the answers are weak.

So I'll swing open each door with a humorous cheer,
And tease out the secrets that tickle my ear.
In this odyssey wild, I may not find a cure,
But I'll laugh through the mysteries, that's for sure!

The Undefined Horizon

The sun sets with a wink,
It dances on the sea,
Questions float like balloons,
Where do they land? Not for me!

A cat walks with a plan,
But loses track of time,
It chases its own tail,
And still thinks it's sublime!

The stars twinkle with glee,
Each one with a tale,
Why do they shine so bright?
It's surely a cosmic fail!

So here we sit and stare,
At things we can't define,
Smiling at the chaos,
In this grand, absurd design.

Musings on the Mystery

A squirrel stole my sandwich,
And then tripped on a tree,
I ponder on the why,
As it blames the birdie.

The clouds above me giggle,
They shift and twirl about,
I ask them for their wisdom,
But they just fluff and pout!

A door creaks in the night,
A ghost? Or just a draft?
I chuckle at the thought,
What happens next? A laugh!

A rubber duck floats by,
In the puddle by my feet,
I wonder who's the captain,
Of this oddball fleet!

The Interplay of Light and Shadow

The lightbulb flickers odd,
Like it's got a joke to tell,
The shadows start to dance,
Oh, how they do it well!

My socks have gone awol,
Did they run off for a thrill?
While my shoes plot a coup,
On a windowsill!

A moth dives for the flame,
It's surely lost its mind,
Is it seeking answers?
Or just a little blind?

The twilight giggles softly,
In whispers dark and fair,
But in this riddle of light,
Who really has a care?

Paths Yet to Be Written

A pathway splits ahead,
With signs all upside-down,
I toss a coin for luck,
And then I wear a frown.

The crickets start a chatter,
Deciding where to leap,
While I'm stuck in between,
Choosing paths—do I peep?

The trees hum their secrets,
In a tune oh-so bizarre,
Wondering who's on first,
In this game of avant-garde.

So grab a hat and smile,
Let's wander without haste,
For what's the point in knowing,
When there's joy to just taste!

Beneath the Surface of Time

Seconds swirl like ice cream cones,
Life's a jester, throwing stones.
Tick, tock, who really cares?
Laughter hides, beneath our glares.

Days leap over time's wide fence,
Chasing thoughts without a sense.
Watch the clock, it winks at me,
What's the point? Just wait and see.

Secrets Woven in Silence

Whispers float on cotton candy,
Truths are sticky, oh so dandy!
Questions hang like laundry lines,
Breezy thoughts, where confusion shines.

Socks mismatched, yet on they stroll,
What's the answer? Who's the fool?
Cupped hands, secrets held so tight,
Maybe ice cream's the true delight.

When Questions Dance in the Dark

Dancing shadows in the night,
Curious critters take to flight.
What's that question? Tap your toe!
Follow whims, let worries go.

Silly questions ring like bells,
Is it a riddle? Only time tells.
Forget the answers, grab a snack,
In the dark, we dance, no lack.

The Unseen Thread of Fate

Threads are pulled in twisted ways,
Fate's a prankster, in a haze.
Tugging gently, round we spin,
Who knew trouble could be such fun?

Yarns unravel, tales unfold,
Seek wise owls, or just be bold.
Life's a quilt of laughter and cheer,
Stitch by stitch, we tame our fear.

The Canvas of What Could Be

With paintbrush in hand, I doodle a dream,
My cat thinks it's lunch, and that's not what it seems.
A purple giraffe dances, all fluffed and plump,
While I trip on my canvas and fall in a lump.

The stars laugh and wink as I go for a glide,
Unraveling truths that I cannot abide.
My hopes are like socks, they disappear too,
Yet I'll keep on creating, with flair and with glue.

Each stroke is a jester in color and jest,
Mixing up answers I can't quite digest.
The canvas keeps changing, it's never the same,
And I chuckle at fate, oh, what a wild game.

Perhaps it's all nonsense, this whimsy I chase,
Still, I paint those wild dreams with a grin on my face.
The laughter we share, in splatters and spills,
Makes the canvas of 'could' a place for the thrills.

Whims of Fate's Design

In a realm where my socks refuse to align,
A squirrel in top hat declares it's just fine.
With a wink and a nod, it juggles my keys,
While I search for lost treasures, like crumbs from a cheese.

Calendars flip, with dates having fun,
They twist and they turn, like a dance in the sun.
"Why don't you check Monday?" my toaster declares,
But Monday feels dusty, like forgotten old wares.

A road not taken leads me to pies,
Where the gnomes share their wisdom, dressed up in disguise.
They laugh at our plans, like a great cosmic jest,
And say, "Just enjoy all this whimsical quest."

With feathers and laughter, we frolic around,
In a whirlwind of chaos, a merry-go-round.
These whims of fate tickle the curious mind,
As I chase the absurd, what wonders I find!

Whispers of the Unseen

Behind closed doors, the secrets will squeak,
An ant in a bowtie has something to speak.
With a wink and a wiggle, it shuffles its feet,
While I ask for the meaning, it serves me a treat.

Whispers of shadows play games on the wall,
A fridge full of laughter, a calendar brawl.
As socks start to dance, and the cat rolls her eyes,
I ponder the riddles in all of their lies.

Invisible fingers pull strings in the night,
While popcorn spills laughter—it's such a delight.
I scribble my thoughts on a napkin of fate,
And wonder just how all the quirks fit in straight.

But maybe it's silly, this riddle I weave,
Like solving a puzzle where none must believe.
With whispers of folly, they swirl and they spin,
I smile with a shrug, as I let the fun in.

Shadows of Truth Unveiled

In the shadows where clues start to mumble and fidget,
A donut debates, "Should I eat or just fidget?"
While pickles discuss with a frog on a shelf,
The meaning of questions we dare not to delve.

A suitcase of giggles lies hidden from view,
While forks and spoons gather for a tea brew.
They toast to the curious, the wacky, the wild,
And the drummers, they chuckle, like a playful child.

Not everything makes sense, and that's just fine,
Like socks in the dryer that dance out of line.
We ponder the shadows while munching on cheese,
And discover that understanding's a jester with ease.

With whispers and winks, the truths will appear,
Amidst the absurd, we find laughter sincere.
So let's tiptoe through moments, both silly and grand,
As the shadows of truth, together we'll stand.

Echoes of the Unanswered

Why do socks always disappear?
They dance in darkness, full of cheer.
The fridge hums secrets in the night,
While spoons debate their flight or fright.

The cat stares hard with knowing eyes,
What's in that box? It's such a surprise!
Questions linger like a bad joke,
Even the goldfish seems to poke.

Beneath a Veil of Dreams

A pillow whispers silly schemes,
Wrapped in blankets of wishes and dreams.
The clock ticks softly, mocking time,
As ducks parade in silly rhyme.

Chairs conspire to move around,
While socks hold secret parties, unbound.
The wall paintings grin at unseen lore,
Each chuckle echoes, begging for more.

The Puzzle of Our Days

Why is cereal always a mystery?
Milk and flakes in a slippery history.
The remote has vanished, who can tell?
Maybe it's hiding in a spell.

Every shoelace ties a new conundrum,
Flip-flops giggle as they come undone.
Goodbye to plans that go awry,
Like pigeons plotting a daring fly.

In the Labyrinth of Choices

What's for dinner? A maze of tastes,
A riddle wrapped in culinary wastes.
The map to socks leads nowhere new,
Each corner turned brings echoes askew.

Coffee cups have their own chatter,
While spoons clash in a gleeful scatter.
With every choice, the fridge holds its breath,
In this comedy, we all dance with death.

The Maze of Existence

In corridors of thought, I roam,
Where socks have vanished, never to come home.
I search for keys that never fit,
As shadowy answers tease and flit.

A jester's laugh, a riddle's twist,
Why do we chase what we can't insist?
Like pizza toppings in a blur,
Is it pineapple or the heart's true spur?

The cat sits smug atop the shelf,
I ask myself if I'm the elf.
Answers hide as if in fright,
While Wi-Fi signals zap our light.

Through all the twists and turns I take,
I ponder which is real, the dream or wake?
As I stumble towards the greatest quest,
I chuckle at the jest of all the stress.

Sketches of the Unrevealed

With crayons bright, I draw my fate,
A stick-figure dance, oh isn't that great?
The clouds are shaped like flying cats,
And burgers bounce atop the mats.

I sketch a road that leads to nowhere,
Where ducks wear hats, a fanciful affair.
What's told in whispers, lost in prose,
Is hidden beneath a clown's bright nose.

The sun wears shades, it's on a break,
While squirrels plot a nutty wake.
In chaos, I find a twisted muse,
For what's the truth if we don't choose?

Every doodle holds a silly clue,
In laughter, seekers find what's true.
With sketches wild and brushes grand,
We seek the answers, made by hand.

Harmonies of the Unsung

In this tune of life, I play off-key,
Serenading dreams held up by glee.
The cat joins in with a meow so proud,
While laundry's lost in a musical crowd.

Who sings the notes that don't exist?
A number of questions in swirling mist.
A sock puppet chorus takes the stage,
As I flip through the chapters of every page.

With a trumpet made of a tinfoil wrap,
I create sounds that burst like a clap.
Is it a symphony or a circus scene?
In the cacophony, I chase my dream.

Each laugh resounds, a playful tune,
As I dance with shadows beneath the moon.
What's true might be just funny lore,
As I step through the open door.

A Glimpse Beyond the Obvious

In a world where questions do the waltz,
I ponder why the cat never halts.
With secret whispers of what's not seen,
I sift through puddles to find the queen.

The breadcrumbs lead, but where to go?
As ducks in bow ties steal the show.
Does wisdom hide beneath a bed?
Or is the truth in what's unsaid?

Beyond the veil of common sense,
I juggle thoughts both dense and tense.
Witty riddles and puns collide,
As I ride the waves of chance and tide.

In every puzzle, there's a jest,
As I twist and twirl through every quest.
To glimpse what's veiled, I laugh and peek,
Finding joy in the absurd and unique.

Whispers of the Unknown

In a garden where cats wear hats,
The sun chuckles at dance of rats.
Why does the turtle cross the road?
To get to the other side unexplored.

The clouds giggle, they float with flair,
While the fish argue, 'Who swims with hair?'
Should we trust a wise old crow?
Or is he a joker in a feathered show?

The moon's a lantern for lost socks,
While clocks get dizzy and try to talk.
Why do penguins waddle so right?
Maybe they're training for a big flight.

In a world where bananas can sing,
Don't ask where the jellybeans spring.
A pickle might just wear a tie,
As the donuts compete in the pie-sky.

Enigmas in the Dawn

The sun yawns loudly, a sleepy sight,
While coffee mugs gossip about the night.
Why does toast always land with a thud?
Is it seeking adventure or just a dud?

The grass whispers secrets to the dew,
While squirrels plan heists with a crew.
Do shadows sneak or just play tricks?
Or do they have plans for a few kicks?

A vacuum cleaner dreams of flight,
Imagining a world filled with light.
Why do umbrellas turn inside out?
Hiding from raindrops without a doubt!

Chickens ponder the mysteries of eggs,
While frogs recite rhymes on their legs.
A cactus juggles while sitting still,
And the moon shakes its head at the thrill.

Shadows of Uncertainty

In a corner where shadows brew,
A toaster debates, 'What's toast to you?'
Why do socks disappear in the wash?
Are they in a party, having a posh?

The goldfish dreams of being a whale,
While ants plan a marvelous trail.
Why do we giggle when life's absurd?
Is it the whispers from a singing bird?

The teapot sighs with a whistle tune,
While stars twinkle, sharing a boon.
Do cookies dance when no one sees?
Or is it just the sugar's tease?

A bicycle wonders about its ride,
While the pencils scribble with pride.
Why do rain boots dance in the puddle?
Is it just joy creating a huddle?

The Riddles of Existence

A pickle and a jelly celebrate their day,
While rubber ducks sing in a bright array.
Why do questions rasp and poke?
Is the punchline hiding from the joke?

The sun wears shades, looking all cool,
While crickets argue who rules the pool.
Do spaghetti strands ever get lost?
Or do they ponder just at all cost?

In the world of mismatched shoes,
Cats plot their own funny stories to choose.
Why do wishes fly after a star?
Is hope just a journey that goes too far?

The moon plays tricks on sleepy eyes,
While balloons float to surprise the skies.
Do time machines ever break down?
Or just take a nap in a whimsical town?

The Questions that Shape Us

Why do cats sit on laptops, it's a truth we seek,
Or why does the toast always land on the floor?
Six socks in the dryer, and they've gone off to speak,
While the fridge gets colder like it's keeping a score.

We ponder the mysteries of food disappearing,
Why does the cereal drown when the milk takes a dive?
Like the lost keys we search for, endless veering,
The answers hide well in the corners, alive.

What makes pigeons gather, plotting a scheme?
Is it a game of tag or a well-done ballet?
Why does ice cream melt faster when kids are extreme?
Such inquiries sparkle like sunbeams in May.

So let's laugh at the riddles that swirl all around,
For seeking the answers is pure comic cheer.
It's the chase that keeps us from easily found,
Those questions we have make the adventure clear.

Expecting the Unexpected

Why does the phone ring when I'm in the shower?
Or why does popcorn pop when it's just for one?
A tornado of last-minute plans brings a flower,
While socks in bright colors confuse everyone.

Each twist of the plot is a ticklish surprise,
Like the prank of a friend with a twist in the tail.
Why do we step on gum, with nothing but sighs?
It's the mystery of fun that we laugh and unveil.

Why do we trip on our own pair of feet?
Why does coffee spill when we rush out the door?
Every moment contains its own funny beat,
Like a cat that sneezes and makes us all roar.

So as we expect what we cannot foresee,
Let's jump into each day, ready for a spin.
For the unexpected is what sets us all free,
With giggles and chuckles, the chaos can win.

Threads of Cosmic Curiosity

Why does the universe sparkle or sometimes just yawn?
Are stars like distant lamps with songs of the night?
Do black holes just party until the dawn?
Am I the only one that thinks this is bright?

I wonder if worms have a secret parade,
Or if aliens watch us, just stuck on a stream.
Are planets just eggs in a cosmic charade?
Do they ever get bored, or dream up a scheme?

What if the moon has a dance of its own?
Or clouds are just pillows for thoughts to collide?
Are raindrops just giggles that don't want to moan?
And laughter is something the sun tries to hide?

So let's weave our wonder with threads of delight,
In this tapestry spun from a wily surprise.
The quirks of the cosmos sparkle ever so bright,
As we chuckle at questions with mischievous eyes.

Illuminated by Curiosity

Why does breakfast taste better when served at noon?
Or why do our shadows start dancing at night?
When socks become burglars, stealing the tune,
And our dreams bring a flicker of giggles in flight.

Is the refrigerator hum a song of despair?
Does the toaster toast faster when we hold our breath?
What if the plants whisper their secrets with flair?
And the ceiling fan thinks it's dodging a death?

Why do pigeons strut like they own the whole street?
Are squirrels just acrobats with nuts in their bag?
What if the books read themselves in the heat?
Should we talk to our shoes before they just lag?

As we wander this maze of whimsical play,
Every question's a puzzle that pulls us apart.
In the glow of our wonder, let's dance and sway,
For curiosity's spark is the light of the heart.

The Cloak of Infinity

Under the stars, I ask my phone,
"What's the meaning?" It just groans.
The universe laughs, it plays its trick,
    Winks at us all, as time does tick.

I asked a cat, it purred and slept,
With wisdom deep, but through it crept,
A hunger for fish, or maybe a mouse,
    Is that the answer to this house?

I pondered hard, then lost my keys,
It seems the cosmos plays with ease.
The coffee's cold; I'm feeling spry,
    Perhaps a donut knows the why?

In tangled webs, confusion spins,
Jerry at work claims he has wins.
But when I checked his lunch today,
A ham sandwich seemed out of play!

Paths Diverged in Mystery

Two roads split in a grassy glade,
One led to ice cream, the other, shade.
I took the risk, chose the sweet,
Found a raccoon, demanding a treat.

A sign proclaimed "This path is wise,"
But it led to pizzas under dark skies.
With olives and cheese, it whispered, "Go!"
But my waistline cried, "Please, no more dough!"

Then came a sage, all dressed in flair,
He sold me fortune cookies, with a stare.
"You'll solve all puzzles by tomorrow noon!"
They just crumbled; sweet cookie doom.

So here I stand, with crumbs galore,
Still lost in thought, forever more.
Paths may merge or wander wide,
But with half-baked answers, who's to decide?

Dreams Wrapped in Enigma

I dreamed last night of a dancing spoon,
Sipping tea with an old raccoon.
He asked me why the moon was round,
I said, "It's full of dreams profound."

A voice echoed from the kitchen shelf,
"You should really ask yourself!"
But then the toaster popped out toast,
It burned a bit, just like my ghost.

Pondering life in a chocolate haze,
My mind got lost in a sugary maze.
I tripped on gum and fell through clouds,
With candy floss wrapped in giggly shrouds.

So if you see a raccoon tonight,
With dreams so sweet and quite a sight,
Remember to ask him the why and where,
But watch your snacks; he's quite a bear!

The Language of Shadows

Shadows dance in the evening light,
Whispering secrets of day and night.
I tried to chat with a shadow near,
It just laughed and disappeared, oh dear!

A lamp post claimed it knew the score,
But all it did was snore and snore.
With every flicker, I'd lose my thought,
Are these clues or just tricks they've bought?

The moon said, "Listen, I float with ease!"
"And by the way, I'm allergic to bees."
It's hard to converse with such glossy dreams,
Especially when reality always beams.

So here I sit with shadows bold,
Trading riddles, or so I'm told.
Grab your lantern, don't trip and fall,
For wisdom's a dance; it shadowed us all!

Unfolding the Hidden Layers

Upon a banana, wisdom I'll propose,
Peeling back layers, nobody knows.
The truth slips out like a wayward sock,
Mysteries dance around the tick-tock.

A parrot tells jokes, who knew he'd be wise?
With feathers so bright and bright, clever lies.
Every riddle wrapped in a squawk and a yawn,
Leaves us awake but still slightly withdrawn.

I asked the goldfish where secrets reside,
In bubbles he giggles, a splash, then he hides.
The depth of the water, so simple, yet grand,
Holds stories and tales too fuzzy to stand.

So grab your magnifying glass, take a peek,
At life's quirky puzzles, it's fun, so to speak.
As we chase the absurd in this curious quest,
Remember, the layers are part of the jest.

Tales of the Unfathomed

A turtle once pondered the speed of the sun,
He laughed and he said, 'That's no way to run!'
The stories we chase swim deep like a fish,
No wonder our whims are granted a wish.

The squirrel debates with the wind in the park,
'Do I jump to my nuts, or stay here in the dark?'
His solutions keep changing with every bright breeze,
While I sip my soda with sticky sweet ease.

An owl gave me wisdom, yet I fell asleep,
His answers were tangled, oh what a heap!
He hooted on riddles, with feathers so sly,
Truths flutter around, but you still can't say why.

So gather your whims, and dance with that doubt,
Each step is a gamble in laughter and clout.
We'll pen down these tales, with a wink and a nod,
For wandering wonders, we'll always applaud.

Wonders Behind Closed Doors

Behind every door, there's a dance and a cheer,
A cat in a top hat sipping vanilla beer.
While socks have a meeting to discuss their fate,
The comedy plays on, and oh, isn't it great?

A cupboard of jesters, they all gather round,
With pie in the face, what a sight to be found!
Their answers are silly but spark such delight,
Who knew that a spoon could tickle at night?

In the closet, a wizard brews magical tea,
He insists it'll help you find the lost key.
But all we discover is laughter and fun,
With secrets so sweet under each funny pun.

So knock on those doors, and let wonders unfold,
In the heart of the curious, there's treasure untold.
With giggles and grins, we'll follow the lore,
The wonders of life are behind every door.

Forgotten Truths of the Heart

A toaster once sighed about love in a way,
'Why is the bread the crumb of the day?'
It burned and it laughed, a charred little joke,
Yet wisdom still peeked from that soft, ashy cloak.

Birds gossip sweet secrets on branches so high,
'What if our dreams are just clouds in the sky?'
They winged and they whirled, with feathers askew,
Leaving whispers of truth that we all wished we knew.

A sock puppet pondered what makes hearts spin fast,
'Is it love that we chase, or shadows we cast?'
With winks from its buttons and stitches so bright,
It danced in the moonlight, a comical sight.

So toast to the puzzled, the laugh that's your start,
In the nooks and the crannies, there's warmth in the heart.

Let's raise our glasses to truths that amuse,
For the funniest fables are what we all choose.

The Unknown's Embrace

In shadows where the giggles hide,
We search for whispers, then we slide.
A sock, a shoe, a chicken's song,
Who knew that nothing could feel so wrong?

There's wisdom in the lost and found,
Where every corner giggles around.
A riddle wrapped in a noodle,
Sriracha kisses, quite the doodle!

A banana peel spills secrets bright,
On floors of dreams, in silly flight.
Like cats that dance on midnight streets,
With ancient truths buried in their tweets.

So here we dance with fate and fate,
In a wobble waltz, oh isn't it great?
We twirl in circles, and sometimes fall,
With laughter echoing, we heed its call.

Echoes of the Unexplored

In forests deep where squirrels jest,
Acorns tumble, like jesters at best.
The trees all whisper forgotten lore,
While mushrooms giggle and mushrooms roar.

The unknown is a capricious friend,
With every twist, a 'wait, what?' blend.
Like socks that vanish, take a peek,
The answers hide, so sly and meek.

A fortune cookie winked at me bold,
Said, 'Life's a joke, just be controlled.'
I laughed so hard, the cookie broke,
Now all I do is crack the yolk.

In mirrors two, I can see the pranks,
Reflection questions, with no thanks.
Embrace the riddle, let it be,
The fun's in not finding, can you see?

The Jigsaw of Tomorrow

A puzzle piece from yesterday,
Stuck in a drawer, it likes to play.
With corners frayed and colors wild,
It dances off, a mischievous child.

The pieces twist, and some are lost,
But finding them isn't worth the cost.
With every turn, a giggle sounds,
As tomorrow's jigsaw twirls around.

So grab a shard and strike a pose,
The jigsaw speaks, but who really knows?
A cat may fit into the sky,
While fish wear hats and birds just sigh.

In bits and bobs, our fate we weave,
A wobbly dance, a gleeful reprieve.
Who needs the answers, come what may?
Let laughter be our guiding way!

Enigma Beneath the Surface

Beneath the waves, the secrets sleep,
With fish in tuxedos, their knowledge deep.
They gather round in swirls of foam,
To plot the course of things unknown.

A crustacean grins, his eyes all bright,
He cracks a joke in the pale moonlight.
What's buried here, what's lost in time?
It's all a riddle, a silly rhyme.

When the tide rolls in with a great big splash,
We marvel at the treasure, the fragile cache.
But each shiny shell has a tale to tell,
Like how a crab may dance, not just dwell.

So dive into the friendly abyss,
With quirks and giggles, it's pure bliss.
Embrace the wave, let mystery steer,
For laughter's the answer, loud and clear!

www.ingramcontent.com/pod-product-compliance
Lightning Source LLC
Chambersburg PA
CBHW071842160426
43209CB00003B/381